I Love
Horses

By Lisa Regan
Illustrated by Ian Jackson

Miles
Kelly

First published in 2008 by Miles Kelly Publishing Ltd
Harding's Barn, Bardfield End Green,
Thaxted Essex, CM6 3PX, UK

This edition printed 2011

2 4 6 8 10 9 7 5 3

Publishing Director Belinda Gallagher
Creative Director Jo Cowan
Editorial Assistant Toby Tippen
Designer Carmen Johnson
Cover Artworker Carmen Johnson
Production Manager Elizabeth Collins
Reprographics Stephan Davis, Ian Paulyn
Assets Lorraine King

ISBN 978-1-84810-045-9

Printed in China

ACKNOWLEDGEMENTS
Page 20 Jürgen Mischke/Fotolia.com
All other images from the Miles Kelly Archives

British Library Cataloguing-in-Publication Data
A catalogue record for this book is available
from the British Library

Made with paper from a sustainable forest

www.mileskelly.net   info@mileskelly.net

www.factsforprojects.com

Contents

Arab

Many people think Arab horses are the most beautiful of all. These horses first came from the hot desert countries of the Middle East. Arabs are very good at running a long way without getting tired.

This horse has big eyes and its ears are small and pointy. The head is narrower at the nose end.

Keep running

An Arab can run for a long time. Use a stopwatch to see how long you can run for before you start to feel tired.

This horse colour is known as chestnut, but Arabs can also be grey or black. They often have white markings called socks on the legs.

4

An Arab horse is easily recognized because it carries its tail high up.

Arabs are friendly horses, but they are usually too lively for people who are learning to ride!

In the stable

Horses are often brought inside to keep them safe, warm and dry. The building where they live is called the stable. All the special equipment used for riding and looking after horses is kept in the stable, too.

Haflinger ponies are always chestnut, with pale-coloured manes and tails.

A saddle and reins are put on a horse before riding it. The saddle is a kind of seat that is comfortable to sit on.

Covering up
Horses and ponies that are kept outside can wear a rug to stay warm and dry.

This Akhal-Teke horse is groomed to make it look beautiful for a show and to keep its skin clean and healthy.

Quarter horse

This saddle allows the cowboy to ride his horse all day long without hurting the horse or the rider.

This horse comes from the United States. It can run very fast over short distances and is often seen in rodeo competitions. Quarter horses are ridden by cowboys.

Cowboy gear

Cowboys wear leather chaps over their trousers. Chaps protect the legs from thorny bushes and cactus plants.

A cowboy is a person who looks after cattle on large American farms called ranches.

A cowboy holds his horse's reins in one hand. His other hand is free to hold his lasso, which is a rope used to catch cows.

This horse is pinto coloured. This means it has large patches of white and one other colour, such as chestnut.

Appaloosa

This horse usually has patterns on its coat. Some have spots, a bit like a leopard! Appaloosas are friendly horses that can be handled easily by people learning to ride.

A bridle is a strap fitted to the horse's head to help the rider keep it under control. It is usually made from leather.

Pony trekking or trail riding is great fun. A group of riders will often ride across fields and up hills all day!

Snow pattern
Dark-coloured horses with white spots on their bodies are said to have a snowflake pattern.

Appaloosas often have stripes on their hooves.

Shire horse

One of the world's biggest horses is the Shire horse. It has long hair at the bottom of its legs that grows over its hooves. Before tractors and trucks were invented, Shire horses were often used to pull heavy carts.

An adult Shire horse weighs about a tonne. That's as much as a family car!

Measuring up

A Shire horse can measure 180 centimetres at its shoulder. That's about the same height as a grown man. How tall are you?

Shire horses are very gentle and patient. They make excellent work horses on farms.

A special neck piece called a harness is used to attach the farm equipment. This helps the horses pull heavy things.

These horses look beautiful when they are dressed up for a show. They wear horse brasses and other decorations.

Connemara

This is a kind of pony that first came from Ireland. Connemaras are very good at jumping and are often chosen by people who want to enter competitions. A Connemara can be ridden by children and adults.

It is important to wear a proper safety hat whenever you ride a horse.

Show jumping is one of the sports at the Olympic Games. The rider has to help the horse jump over different obstacles.

Prize winners

The winners of horse-riding competitions are given a special ribbon called a rosette.

A sandy-coloured horse is called dun. Some dun horses also have stripes on their legs.

Ponies are trained at a very young age. They are taught to be well-behaved when being ridden.

Shetland

The Shetland pony is very small.
At the shoulder, it is the same height as a four-year-old child. These ponies have long, shaggy coats to keep them warm in cold weather.

Shetland ponies are usually kept as pets, but they are sometimes used to pull a small carriage.

Danger diet
Horse owners must be very careful of what their horses eat. Some plants, such as acorns, are poisonous.

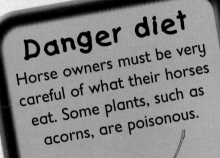

A baby horse is called a foal. Foals can stand up before they are even one day old!

An adult Shetland has a very long mane and tail.

A pony's fringe is called its forelock. Shetland ponies have a forelock that covers their eyes.

Falabella

This is a tiny horse, as small as some types of dog! Falabellas are kept as pets, and are very friendly and loving to their owners. In competitions, they have to be led around the ring on a rope.

Because they are so small, and not very strong, Falabellas can only be ridden by children.

This horse is trotting next to its owner. A horse can also walk, canter and gallop.

Falabellas were originally bred in Argentina, a country in South America.

New shoes

A horse or pony is taken to a farrier to have horseshoes made and fitted to its hooves.

Camargue

These horses often live in wild groups called herds. They are very strong, and are well-suited to living in wet, marshy areas. Camargues are very sure-footed so they can be ridden on rough, bumpy ground without tripping or falling.

Rounded up

Farm workers called gardiens use Camargues to round up wild black bulls.

As they grow older, Camargue horses get paler. When they are born, they can be black or dark brown.

Camargue foals stay close to their mothers for up to two years. They then start looking for a mate.

Broad hooves help the horses run across wet land, or even in the sea. As they live in the wild, they don't wear horseshoes.

Friesian

This jet-black horse is strong and elegant. The Friesian's colour and graceful trotting style makes it perfect for pulling carriages at weddings and funerals. It is also used a lot in films.

Friesians come from an area called Friesland in the Netherlands, which is a country in Europe.

Silky hair on the lower legs is called feathering. It is often kept long to make horses look smart in competitions.

As they are friendly and easy to handle, Friesians are sometimes used for pony trekking.

Friesians are well known for having long, thick manes and tails.

Long ago
The first type of horse was about the same size as a pet cat. It had toes instead of hooves!

Fun facts

Arab Whatever the colour of an Arab horse's coat, the skin is always black underneath.

Quarter horse To help a cowboy round up cattle on a ranch, a Quarter horse must be able to stop, start and turn very quickly.

Appaloosa Paintings on cave walls show that spotted horses lived thousands of years ago.

Shire horse This horse is so strong that it is able to pull up to fives times its own weight!

Connemara These ponies are are very tough. They are used to living in cold, wet and windy weather.

Shetland Being small makes it easier for Shetland ponies to find shelter.

Falabella Although it may seem like a pony because it is so small, a Falabella is actually a rare breed of miniature horse.

Camargue There is only poor quality food available to Camargues in the wild. They must live off whatever grass and plants they can find.

Friesian Nearly all Friesians are completely black, but some have a small white star on their foreheads.